This book belongs to

_____

Charlie and His Lost Friend

Copyright © 2015 by Layne Case

ISBN: 978-0-692376-04-1
Library of Congress PCN 2015901481

Inquiries should be addressed to:
AMITY Publications
37 Rogers Run
Barrington, NH 03825

To contact Layne Case or to order a copy of this book, please visit
www.amitypublications.com

Design and Layout by
Nancy Grossman
www.nancygrossmanbooks.com

Printed in the United States of America

Charlie
and
His Lost Friend

Written by Layne Case
Illustrated by Lorena Mary Hart

In Memory of my Mom – Gloria M. Pitocchelli

It was a beautiful summer day in a small town in New Hampshire.   Charlie loved to walk around his neighborhood, making sure all his neighbors and friends were safe.

Charlie is a little dog. He has big floppy ears, skinny legs, huge paws and a three-foot-long tail! At first, most who meet Charlie only notice his tail. But, they soon learn what a wonderful dog he is and how his tail has helped so many others.

Charlie was born in New Orleans, Louisiana, just around the time of Hurricane Katrina. It was one of the worst storms ever. Many families lost everything and ended up relocating to other areas.

That is how Charlie came to live in New Hampshire.

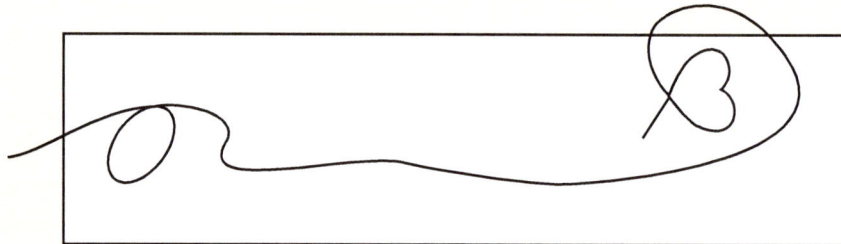

Charlie loved his new home but he missed his friends in New Orleans, especially Lucky.

He never knew what happened to Lucky. One day they were playing together. The next day, everything was destroyed. He never saw Lucky again.

Charlie did have lots of new friends in his neighborhood.

There was Louie, the lizard. He lived right next door to Charlie.

There was Meisha, Mia, Misty and Meezer, the Siamese cats who lived across the street.

And, there was Bruno. He lived down in the cul de sac. Bruno was a pretty big dog. He and Charlie were often seen walking up and down the streets, making sure everything was okay.

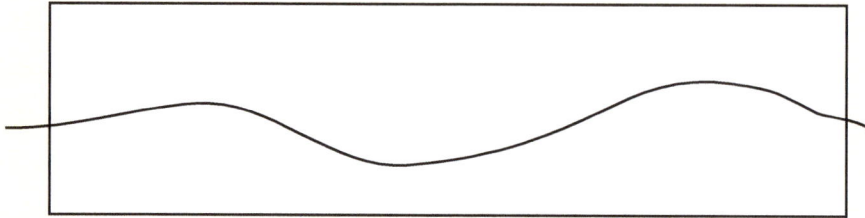

One day, Charlie learned there was a new dog in the neighborhood. He'd overheard his family talking about the neighbors, Todd and Tiffini Walker's new dog. It seems he was adopted from a rescue shelter.

So, Charlie headed out to try to find
this new dog. He thought it would
be great to introduce him to all his
friends and make him feel welcomed.

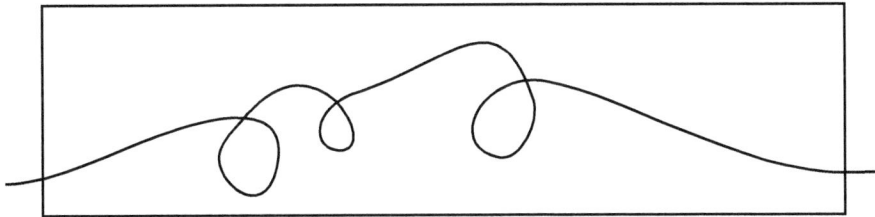

Just as Charlie came to the end of his driveway, he noticed a big dog standing in the middle of the road just a ways down the road. He was looking right at Charlie, growling and baring his teeth.

Charlie stopped, not knowing if he should continue on. He decided, as scary as this dog seemed, he would show him he wanted to be his friend.

As Charlie got closer, he could see the dog a little clearer. He sure was different.

One ear was partially missing. He was pretty scruffy looking with a few scars on his legs and body.

He did *not* look very friendly.

The dog began to walk toward Charlie, growling louder and louder. Charlie wondered if he should growl back to show him he wasn't scared. But, he really *was* afraid. He thought maybe he might just turn around and run home. But, he didn't want to do that either.

So, he decided to use kindness in hopes of befriending this new dog. As the dog starting walking toward Charlie, Charlie began to shake, wondering if he was making the right decision to stay put.

"Hello," Charlie said softly. "Welcome to the neighborhood. I heard you just moved in."

The dog continued to growl at Charlie. He wasn't about to let his guard down. He would show Charlie who was in charge.

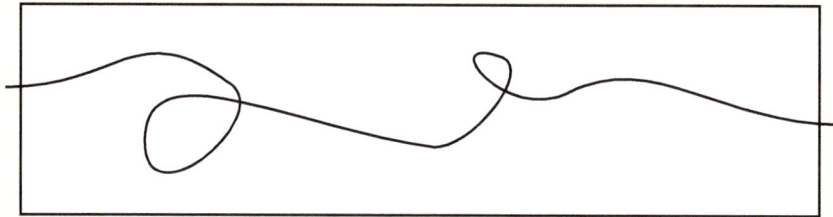

Charlie continued. "My name is Charlie. What's your name?"

For a moment, the dog stopped growling. Could he trust this "Charlie" dog? Could this dog be ... his friend? No way! Never again would he trust anyone.

"I'm Tucker and I'm not looking for any friends," Tucker said fiercely.

Charlie stood his ground. "Well, I just wanted to welcome you and introduce you to some of my friends." Tucker growled. Charlie continued, "So, where did you come from?"

Tucker hesitated for a moment. He was embarrassed to share that he had been living in a rescue shelter. His family had dropped him off one day and never even said goodbye.

"My family had to move and couldn't take me with them," Tucker explained. "But, it wasn't because they didn't love me," he quickly added. "They did! They..."

Tucker stopped. Tears welled up in his eyes, but he continued. "They thought it was best for me to live with another family."

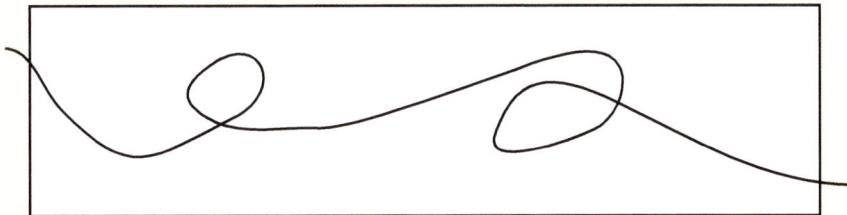

Charlie could see the pain in Tucker's eyes. He also realized something else. It almost felt as if he'd met Tucker before. But that was impossible.

Charlie would have remembered a dog like Tucker. He had lots of scars. Charlie wondered how Tucker got them.

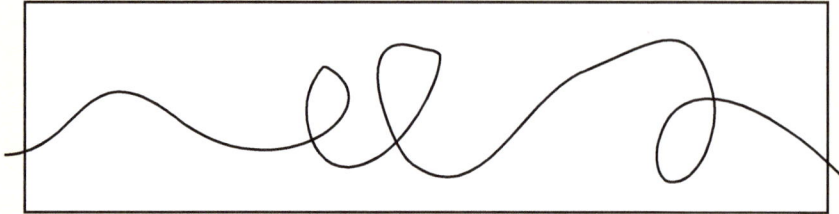

Before Charlie could respond, Tucker growled again.

"I'm not interested in being friends with you or anyone else," Tucker said. "Just leave me alone. And stay out of my territory."

Charlie was shocked. *His* territory? Who did this dog think he was?

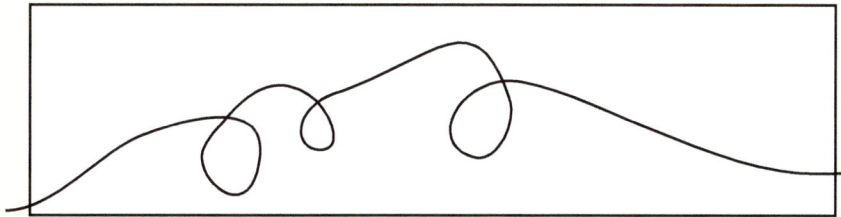

This neighborhood didn't belong to anyone. It was everybody's neighborhood.

Charlie had all he could do not to challenge Tucker. He decided not to react to Tucker's angry threat and turned around, heading back home.

He looked back and said, "Well, Tucker. Still want to welcome you to the neighborhood."

Days went by before Charlie ventured outside again. He was afraid he might meet up with Tucker. Charlie was not the kind of dog who liked to fight. He just wanted to be friends.

Finally, Charlie decided he couldn't allow Tucker to keep him inside. He really missed all his friends.

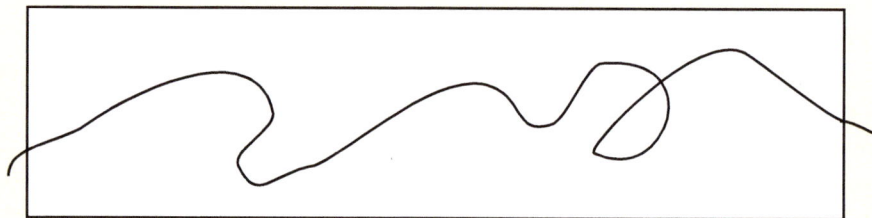

So, Charlie headed out. He hadn't gone very far when he heard someone crying out. It was coming from Tucker's back yard.

Oh, dear, thought Charlie. What am I going to do? He didn't want to "trespass" on Tucker's property, especially after the threat the other day.

Charlie heard the crying again, this time sounding more desperate, almost like a howl. He started to walk toward the sound. It was coming from the woods near the brook.

As Charlie got closer, he saw Tucker sitting on a rock in the middle of the brook. He looked very frightened.

When Tucker saw Charlie, he began yelling for help.

Charlie yelled out, "Tucker, the brook isn't very deep. Just dog paddle to the edge."

Tucker shouted, "I can't swim and, umm, I'm really afraid of water."

Charlie was surprised. Every dog could dog paddle. And, Tucker? Afraid of water?

Charlie thought for a moment, then, yelled back. "Tell you what. My tail is three feet long and very strong. I'll toss it out to you so you can grab on to it. Then, I'll pull you to shore."

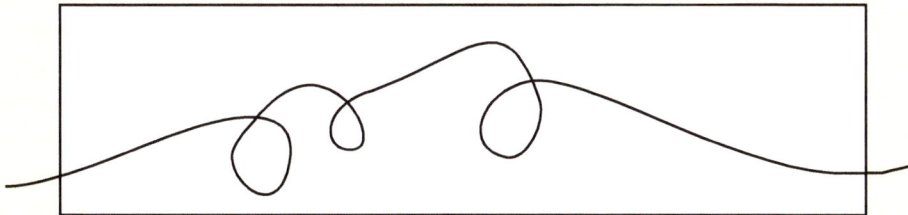

Charlie tossed his tail to Tucker who grabbed on to it with his teeth. Charlie yelped! Tucker was so afraid, he didn't realize how hard he had bitten down.

Charlie decided to endure the pain and get Tucker to the shore as quickly as possible.

Once back on shore, Tucker shook himself dry. He looked up at Charlie, trying to cover up his fear. After all, he was the mean dog in the neighborhood everyone avoided. He didn't want or need any friends. He liked being by himself.

Charlie looked at Tucker. It was clear he had been really scared. Charlie hoped he could show Tucker he wanted to be his friend.

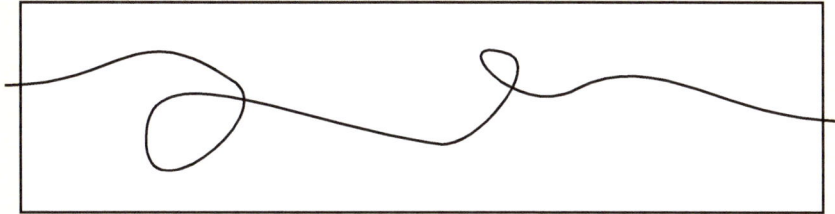

"Tucker? Are you okay? I realize being new to the neighborhood, you wouldn't know Mallego Brook isn't very deep," said Charlie.

Tucker was really embarrassed. Fact was, the brook wasn't deep at all. Tucker could have walked from the rock to the shore. But his fear of water made it impossible.

Tucker did all he could not to cry. He was really lonely and wanted to have a friend. But, the last time he got close to someone, they abandoned him. Not only had he lost his family but his best friend, too.

Tucker liked Charlie, even if he was different from other dogs Tucker had met. Big floppy ears, skinny legs, big paws. And, that tail! Very strange. However, Tucker wasn't all that good looking either. After all those years of fighting, he had scars to prove it.

Charlie looked at Tucker and said quietly "Tucker. I'm not sure why you are so angry. But, I would really like to be your friend."

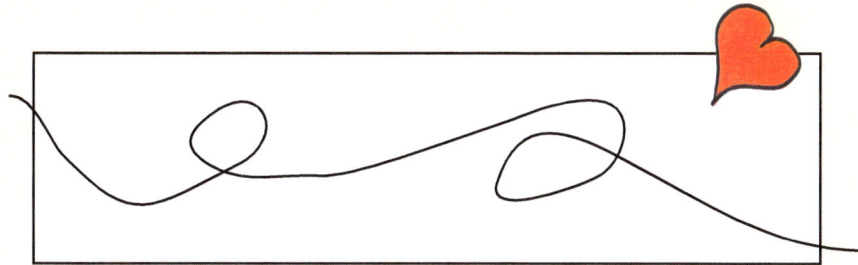

Tucker put his head down. He had started to cry and didn't want Charlie to see. But, he wanted a friend again.

So, he decided to share his story.

"When I was young," he told Charlie, "I lived in New Orleans. One morning, a hurricane hit land and my family lost everything. They put me in a shelter while they tried to rebuild their home. But, they never came back to get me."

Tucker went quiet for a moment, then continued, "And my best friend left without saying goodbye. I was really angry. I started fighting with all the other dogs at the shelter. The owners of the shelter separated me from the other dogs. I spent many long days by myself."

It wasn't easy for Tucker, but he kept on with his story. "One day, Todd and Tiffini came to the shelter and adopted me. Oh, they try to be loving and kind, but I know eventually they'll abandon me, just like my other family, and my best friend ... Charlie. I made a decision back then," Tucker said grimly, "not to get close to anyone ever again."

Charlie couldn't believe what he was hearing. He knew he had recognized something about Tucker the first day they met.

"Tucker! It's me! Charlie! From New Orleans. Only … when we lived there, your name was Lucky!" Charlie exclaimed.

Tucker's eyes opened wide. "Charlie? Charlie Whittney? Really? Is that you?" he asked.

"It sure is, my friend," said Charlie, wagging his tail, jumping up and down.

Tucker and Charlie spent the next four hours catching up. Charlie apologized for not saying goodbye. He had no idea he was moving after Hurricane Katrina.

Tucker and Charlie decided that the past, difficult as it was, would not affect their future together. So, they picked up where their friendship had left off.

Charlie introduced Tucker to all his friends.

At first, Louie was really afraid of Tucker.
He wasn't a very friendly looking dog.

Meisha kept her babies close to her in case
Tucker tried to bite them.

Tucker tried to show them he just wanted
to be their friend.

Bruno stood next to Tucker, making sure Tucker understood Bruno was the neighborhood watch dog.

When Tucker made it clear he would not challenge Bruno, Bruno asked Tucker to join him and Charlie when they walked around the neighborhood. Tucker was honored.

Now the neighborhood would be even safer than ever before.

From Todd and Tiffani Ferris, Tucker's parents:

Tucker was only a few weeks old when he was found in the woods of South Carolina. He was brought to New Hampshire by "Wooffun" (www.wooffun.com) and determined to be about eight weeks old, so we determined his birthday to be June 8, 2010. Tucker is a boxer and ??? mix. He was a bit nervous, liked to eat twigs, sticks and acorn covers, and tended to pounce rather than walk.

Today, Tucker is still a bit nervous, but he's more like Eeyore from the book *Winnie, the Pooh*. He's rather lazy, doesn't like to give kisses and likes to be by himself. He isn't very motivated by food. However, he does look forward to his favorite weekend donut. He enjoys being outside, pretending to sleep under the shrubs while he watches people walking by—he loves to greet them. His brother, Tully, who is now three years old, arrived in March 2012. Tucker and Tully are typical brothers, although Tully does tend to boss his older brother around.

Tucker

Tucker and Tully

Tucker waiting for his donut

Todd & Tiffini Ferris, Tucker's family

History of Hurricane Katrina

Resource: www.history.com/topics/hurricane-katrina

Early in the morning on August 29, 2005, Hurricane Katrina struck the Gulf Coast of the United States. When the storm made landfall, it had a Category 3 rating on the Saffir-Simpson Hurricane Scale—it brought sustained winds of 100–140 miles per hour, and stretched some 400 miles across.

The storm itself did a great deal of damage, but its aftermath was catastrophic. Levee breaches led to massive flooding, and many people charged that the federal government was slow to meet the needs of the people affected by the storm. Hundreds of thousands of people in Louisiana, Mississippi and Alabama were displaced from their homes, and experts estimate that Katrina caused more than $100 billion in damage. Katrina pummeled huge parts of Louisiana, Mississippi and Alabama, but the desperation was most concentrated in New Orleans. Before the storm, the city's population was mostly black (about 67 percent); moreover, nearly thirty percent of its people lived in poverty. Katrina exacerbated these conditions, and left many of New Orleans's poorest citizens even more vulnerable than they had been before the storm.

In all, Hurricane Katrina killed nearly 2,000 people. Hundreds of thousands of evacuees scattered far and wide. Today, after years of recovery and rebuilding efforts, people along the Gulf Coast have made great strides in returning to life as usual even as they continue to rebuild.

From Juli Juneau
A resident of New Orleans and friend of the author

"I've seen New Orleans grow and change since 1990. Of course, Hurricane Katrina was a devastating experience for all of us. Ten years later, we are still rebuilding homes, schools, hospitals, streets and neighborhoods.

"We are grateful for our characters and our musicians who again fill the streets and bubble up from our unique blend of cultures and history in the French quarter. We value our Mardi Gras Indians now more than ever, and are still helping them to rebuild their stockpiles of feathers and beads to make their yearly Indian 'suits.' We still rejoice when another one of us moves back to New Orleans after their Katrina exile. That experience brought us all closer together. We now have a history, a shared experience that we overcame as a city, as a people, and as individuals. We were blessed to have seen our value reflected back to us in the enormous outpouring of emotion and aid that came from everyone in the United States and around the world.

"Hurricane Katrina bonded us forever. We now know if we could overcome Katrina, we can overcome anything. We are resilient."

Juli is a glass artist and the owner of **Nomad Collection** (www.nomadcollection.com), the co-founder of the **Housing and Education Foundation** (www.hefcorp.org) and **The Lake Juneau Safari Park** in Avoyelles Parish, LA.

The End

www.ingramcontent.com/pod-product-compliance
Lightning Source LLC
LaVergne TN
LVHW072119070426
835511LV00002B/23